BOOK 8

NANCY CLANCY
Late-Breaking News!

BOOK 8

NANCY CLANCY

Late-Breaking News!

WRITTEN BY
Jane O'Connor

ILLUSTRATIONS BY
Robin Preiss Glasser

HARPER
An Imprint of HarperCollinsPublishers

ISBN 978-0-06-226972-0
Typography by Jeanne L. Hogle
18 19 20   BRR   10 9 8 7 6 5
❖
First paperback edition, 2018

For Joelle, the newest member of our family!

—J.O'C.

For Vicky and Marty, with love

—R.P.G.

CONTENTS

NOT MUCH NEWS

"The *Gazette*! It's here!" Nancy and Bree shouted out as they hopped off their bikes. They both were waving the latest issue of the *Third Grade Gazette*.

Nobody was in the backyard to hear them. Still Nancy kept shouting "The

1

Gazette! The *Gazette*!" simply because it was fun to say. A gazette was the same thing as a newspaper but sounded much more elegant and French.

Bree beat Nancy to the clubhouse and settled into the hammock they'd recently rigged up. So Nancy plunked down on the beanbag chair. She opened the *Gazette* and skimmed the pages.

"Here it is," she said, disappointed. Her article was on the last page and didn't take up much space. Nancy was not surprised.

BIG MENU CHANGES COMING YOUR WAY

by Nancy Clancy

Next month, the Ada M. Draezel Elementary School cafeteria will change Thursday menus to salads only. According to the school dietician, Mr. Anastas, "This is part of our ongoing effort to serve students more nutritious food."

"I wanted to uncover big news," she said to Bree. "All I got was salads." Nancy sighed. "At least it was printed." Nancy's last story—about two kids getting nosebleeds after accidently banging into each other during recess—had not. And her headline had been superb: "Gore in the School Yard! Blood Everywhere!"

Bree looked up. She had been reading the *Gazette* while swaying back and forth in the hammock. "Nothing in here is big news. See what's on the front page."

Under the headline "Fun at the Planetarium" was a story about a recent class trip. "This doesn't even count as news."

Bree went on. "Not when you stop to think about it."

"True," Nancy replied. After all, the whole third grade had been on the trip. So everyone already knew about the IMAX show on stars and the meteor exhibit.

"The problem is you can't make news happen," Bree said, and shrugged. "We might as well face it. Most third graders don't lead exciting lives."

Even though Bree was correct, that was exactly what Nancy didn't want to face. She wanted life—even for nine-year-olds— to be bursting with thrilling news.

"Your column looks great," Nancy said, feeling a pang of envy. What Bree had written took up half a page.

"Merci beaucoup."

Unlike Nancy and most of the other kids, Bree wasn't a reporter. Instead she wrote an advice column called "Just Ask Bree." Kids sent in their problems to her anonymously. That meant they didn't sign their real name. In this issue Bree answered a letter from a kid who hadn't been invited to a birthday party. The letter was from "Left Out."

"Your answer to Left Out is sensible and understanding," Nancy said admiringly.

Dear Left Out,

Do something extra fun that day with a friend who isn't going to the party either. That way neither of you will be thinking about what you're missing. And try to remember that nobody gets invited to every single party.

Bree

"*Merci beaucoup* again," Bree said. Then she hoisted herself out of the hammock. "Here. Your turn. I'm getting dizzy."

As they traded places, Nancy thought to herself how lucky she was to have Bree for her best friend. If something was bothering her, Nancy never needed to write to

Bree and wait ages until the next *Gazette*
came out for an answer. Bree lived right
next door. Nancy could get superb advice
whenever she needed.

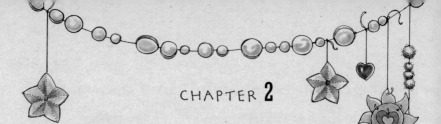

CHAPTER 2

STRANGE TURN OF EVENTS

Later, after Bree went home, Nancy found her parents at the kitchen table. They were trying to do work. It had to be hard with JoJo chasing Frenchy around and around with a lasso.

Papers were strewn all over the table-top—bank statements, tax returns, and

9

lots of bills—the kind of stuff that made being a grown-up seem so dreary to Nancy.

"*Voilà*—the latest issue of the *Gazette*." Nancy presented her parents with the copy. They looked up and smiled.

"I wrote one of the articles. But I have to admit, it's pretty boring."

"Great, sweetie. Can't wait to read it," her mother said in a distracted way. She went back to staring at a bunch of numbers on the screen of her laptop while nibbling on a saltine cracker. Lately Nancy's mother had little appetite and seemed to live on saltine crackers. Every trip to the super- market, she'd stock up on more.

"JoJo, honey, could you please chase Frenchy somewhere else?" Nancy's mom said, sounding tired. Then she looked at her watch. "Whoops. Almost dinnertime. Doug, put in the casserole, okay?"

Nancy's dad stood and walked over to the fridge, still focused on a sheet of paper he'd been examining. "Well, I suppose we could hold off trading in the car," he said, almost as if talking to himself. "And maybe this summer we only stay a week at the cottage."

"*Sacre bleu!*" Nancy said. In French that meant "Yipes!" "Did you just say what I think you said?"

Every July her family spent two weeks at the beach in a rented house. It was the highlight of the Clancys' summer. Why would her parents want to cut down on fun? Then it hit her. "Wait a second. Did we get poorer? Are we in financial difficulty?"

"No. No. Absolutely not. Scout's honor."
Her father raised his hand in the Boy
Scout salute.

"Dad wants to work from home," Nancy's
mom explained.

Suddenly JoJo stopped whizzing around
the table. "Daddy will stay home every
day?" She looked
puzzled.

"Yes. That's
the idea," he
said.

"Goody!" JoJo threw her arms around her father's legs.

"So we're figuring out if we can make ends meet," Nancy's dad went on. "And it looks like we can."

"Oh! I see." Nancy stopped to mull over the brand-new idea of a stay-at-home dad.

Ever since she could remember, her dad had worked downtown for Castle Accountants. They did tax returns for people. Sometimes there were ads on TV. They always ended with a man in a crown saying, "Tax time is never a hassle when you come into Castle."

"Daddy!" JoJo exclaimed. "It'll be so much fun. You can watch *Cowgirl Sal* every day!"

"The very first thing I thought of!" Nancy's

dad told JoJo. Then he turned to Nancy. "I won't have to fight traffic every day. If I need to leave work early, I can because I'll be my own boss! And—" A blissful smile crossed her father's face. "I can live in a T-shirt and sweatpants."

"Dad, I think it's a superb idea!" Nancy said. "Go for it!" She was glad for her dad. She wanted him to be happier. And she was even gladder to know her family wasn't in financial difficulty.

* * *

After finishing her homework, Nancy still had an hour before bedtime, an hour to read. She was in the middle of a Nancy Drew book, and nothing went better with a good mystery than a couple of cookies.

Downstairs, in the kitchen, as she

opened the pantry door, Nancy happened to notice something on the floor. It was under the kitchen table. A leaflet of some kind.

Nancy picked it up.

On the front were photos of houses, all of them brand-new and bigger than the one Nancy lived in.

"Find the home of your dreams," it said in big letters at the top. "At Crystal Lake

Estates, you won't just be buying a house. You'll be joining a community."

Puzzled, Nancy turned the leaflet over and read more. "Here at Crystal Lake Estates, your family will enjoy many amenities." There were photographs of a pool, a playground, and a fitness club. Nancy had never heard the word "amenities" before but she guessed it meant fancy extras—like the pool.

Suddenly Nancy felt goose bumps all over, as if she had plunged into a pool of ice-cold water. Why did her parents have this leaflet? Was this the reason her parents were looking at how much money they had? Maybe they weren't only thinking about Dad working at home. Maybe her parents wanted to move!

In a flash, Nancy dashed upstairs and stormed into her parents' room. They were reading in bed.

"I found this in the kitchen!" Nancy waved the leaflet at them. "You don't want to move, do you?"

Her parents exchanged glances.

"It's something Mom and I have talked

about a little bit," her father admitted. "It's just a possibility. A remote possibility. Not all the houses at Crystal Lake are even built yet. So there's no need for you to go and start packing." Her father was trying to make a joke.

"Dad, this isn't funny. You mean moving is even a maybe?" Nancy felt herself sink down on their bed. "I wasn't supposed to see this leaflet, was I?"

Her parents avoided answering the question.

"If Dad is going to be home all the time, we need more space," her mom said. "He needs his own office. . . . And you'd have a huge room with your own private bathroom. Wouldn't that be great?" Her mother's smile scared Nancy. It was the "be reasonable" smile. The smile she used for coaxing JoJo into doing something she didn't want to.

"No! I like it right here." Then Nancy blinked. "Wait. Have you already been out to Crystal Lake Estates? Without JoJo and me?"

"No, no. Of course not," her dad said.

Nancy folded her arms, unconvinced. "Then how do you know I'd have such a big bedroom?"

Her dad turned to her mom. "Why do I feel like we're under investigation?" Then he said to Nancy, "They emailed us floor plans." Her dad reached for the laptop on the nightstand. "Want to see?"

"No! I do not!" Nancy was practically shouting.

"Sweetie, please don't get upset." Her mom leaned over to hug Nancy, but she pulled away.

"Nothing, I repeat, nothing, is settled," her dad said.

"Well, that's good, because I think moving is an awful idea. No. It's worse than awful. It's horrendous."

Nancy marched out of their room and into hers, which—as far as she was concerned—was the perfect size.

The Nancy Drew book was lying on her bed. But Nancy was too upset to read. How foolish she had been. Just this afternoon she had complained how there was never any real news. Now there was—or might be—and she didn't like it one bit.

She had to let Bree know right away

about this horrible development.

Nancy whipped out a notepad and wrote, *Help! We may move!* She wrote it in pig Latin. *Elp-hay e-way ay-may ove-may!* Lately that was how they were keeping messages to each other secret. Nancy rang the bell to signal that their Special Delivery mail basket was on its way over to Bree.

Nancy flopped on her bed and waited

for an answer.

It didn't take long.

Nancy heard Bree's bell and reeled in the basket. Bree was standing by her window. She ran two fingers down her cheeks

to show Nancy how sad she was.

Bree's message said, *This is a big problem. But stay calm. Let me sleep on it.*

＊ ＊ ＊

The next morning, Bree already had come up with a plan. On the way to school, she said, "Okay. So what if you let JoJo share your room? Then JoJo's room could be your father's office."

A shudder ran through Nancy. Although it was small, Nancy's room was her domain. A place that was entirely hers. It was decorated exactly the way she liked, with everything exactly where she wanted it to be. "But we'd need to get bunk beds. My bed would have to go." Nancy had made a canopy for it out of a sheet, a mop, and a broom. "And there'd be JoJo's dumb stuff all over." Posters of Cowgirl Sal and her sidekick, Ramblin' Roy. Nancy shuddered again.

They had reached school. While they parked their bikes, Bree said, "It's not an ideal solution. I know that. But so far it's all I've come up with. Last night I hardly slept. I kept thinking about you moving away." Bree bit her lower lip. "I couldn't stand it. What would I do without you next door?"

Nancy and Bree clasped hands. They didn't speak. There was no need to. They were both thinking the exact same thing— there couldn't be better best friends on the entire planet!

＊ ＊ ＊

"Dudes, you should be very proud of the last issue of the *Gazette*," Mr. Dudeny told the class during social studies. "I read it from cover to cover as soon as I got home."

"How long did that take? Five minutes?"

Grace said, twiddling a pencil on her desk. "It's not like it's a real newspaper—it's only four pages."

Mr. Dudeny ignored the remark. His eyes traveled around the room. "So. Did any of the articles tell you something you hadn't known before?"

Nancy's hand shot up. So did Robert's.

"Okay, Robert, let's hear from you."

Robert said, "I had no idea before I read the *Gazette* how our school got its name."

That was exactly what Nancy was going to say.

The story had been written by Lionel. Ada M. Draezel had been born in their town. It turned out that long ago she had won an Olympic medal for beach volleyball.

"I didn't even know that was an Olympic

sport," Nancy added.

At the beach she went to every summer, it seemed that teenage girls played volleyball mostly to show off in their bikinis.

Clara said, "Lionel, when I saw you wrote the article, part of me wondered if you made everything up. . . . You didn't, did you?"

Lionel acted shocked. "Make it up? How could you think that?"

"Because you're a big goofball," Clara giggled. "You're always pranking people."

Lionel scowled and blew through his lips. "I happen to be a serious journalist. I spent hours digging through old records down at Town Hall to get the facts."

Bree cocked an eyebrow. "Really?"

"*Wel-l-l,* maybe I didn't exactly go down to Town Hall . . . maybe it was more like I Googled Ada M. Draezel. Still." Lionel raised a pointed finger. "I stand by every word I wrote. It's the truth, the whole truth, and nothing but the truth, so help me . . ."

"Got it, Lionel," Mr. Dudeny broke in. "None of us doubts your journalistic integrity. But Clara, the question you raised is important." Mr. D looked around at everyone in the room. "Don't believe everything you read—or hear. If something doesn't sound true, maybe it isn't."

Grace was waving her arm like crazy. So Mr. D called on her.

"I don't think the class trip belonged on the front page," she said.

"Well, thanks a bunch," Nola said. She had written the article.

"It's not news," Grace said. "We all were there."

Sacre bleu! Nancy shot a look at Bree. She knew Bree was thinking the same thing. For once they agreed with Grace!

"I see your point," Mr. D said. "But a newspaper offers more than breaking news. It's also a record of events. That means it reports on what has already happened." Then Mr. D discussed other reasons for reading a newspaper. He brought up Bree's advice column, as well as a movie review by Robert, and Clara's recipe in "Cooking with Clara." Nancy's salad story, alas, went unmentioned.

"I'm not showing my grandma the *Gazette*," Clara told Mr. D. "It's her biscuit recipe and it's supposed to be a secret."

The bell for recess rang.

"Hold it." Mr. D made a stop motion with his hand. "One last thing before you rush out. You never know. There could be news right under your nose. So stay alert and be prepared to report on it."

CHAPTER 3

BREE HAS A PLAN

One of the many things Nancy admired about Bree was her diligence. She was very hardworking. Sure enough, by the end of the school day, Bree had come up with another plan so the Clancys wouldn't have to move. A much better plan than the JoJo one.

31

Nancy ran it by her parents that evening. She waited until her sister had gone to sleep because she wanted her parents' full, undivided attention. She sat them down in the living room. Nancy's mother had a glass of water next to her and a plate of crackers. She hadn't eaten much dinner. Nancy felt bad. Maybe the idea of moving was upsetting her mother too.

"So." Nancy pressed her hands together. "I've been thinking about what you said— how we need more space. I understand. And I have an idea." Nancy paused.

"I'm all ears," her dad said.

"What if I move into Bree's house?"

"What?!" her dad exclaimed.

Her mom didn't say anything. She couldn't because she was coughing. Bits of cracker flew from her mouth.

"Just hear me out. Please," Nancy said, once her mom drank more water and stopped coughing. "This isn't a crazy idea. There's an extra bedroom at Bree's house. The guest room. Nobody uses it."

"And Bree's parents?" her mom asked. "What do they have to say about this?"

"Well, actually, Bree hasn't brought it up with them yet. I wanted to run it by you first." Nancy and Bree had figured out how Nancy could set everything up so her new room would look nearly identical to her room now. Exactly the same. Canopy bed and all.

While she spoke, her dad kept shaking his head. He didn't look angry. He looked amused.

That was a bad sign.

"But I'd be right next door," Nancy pointed out. "I'd still come over here all the time."

"Well, that's reassuring to know."

"Dad, I'm being serious. You could have my room for your office. I'd eat all my meals here—well, maybe not breakfast if

I was in a rush for school."

"Nancy, this is a ridic—"

Nancy didn't let her mother go any further. "Think about it, Mom. At night is when you wouldn't see me. And that's when we're all asleep. You don't see me anyway." But the more she talked, the more Nancy could tell it was a hopeless cause.

"Couldn't Bree at least ask?"

"No, sweetie. She can't."

"But why, Mom?"

"Because we're a family. We don't want you to be a part-time daughter. We want to all live together."

"Under one roof," her father added.

And that was that. Period. End of discussion.

CHAPTER **4**

NO NEWS IS GOOD NEWS

There was more unsettling news on Sunday.

Her mother announced in an overly cheerful voice, "We're going on a fun outing!"

That was not true. The Clancys were driving out to Crystal Lake Estates.

"Just for a look. That's all," her dad kept insisting. "Nothing's signed in blood."

Nancy was torn. Part of her wanted to stay home. Seeing the houses at Crystal Lake Estates would make the idea of moving seem more real. That was frightening. But in the end she went along. Reason one: Bree had to visit relatives and would be away all day. Reason two: Nancy was a tiny bit curious about what all the amenities looked like.

The drive seemed to take forever. "Are we even in the same state?" Nancy asked glumly.

"In fact, if we do move to Crystal Lake Estates—and that's a very big *if*—we'd still be in the same school district. You'd still go to Draezel."

Her mother meant this to be reassuring. But Nancy had never considered the possibility that her parents might move someplace so far away, she'd have to switch schools. Suddenly the granola she'd eaten for breakfast turned over in her tummy.

"I guess we're here," her dad said as a billboard for Crystal Lake Estates finally

came into view. It showed the same house and happy family pictured on the leaflet.

"Oh no!" her mother said, blinking. "I don't believe this."

As everyone piled out of the car, Nancy understood why her mother sounded dismayed.

Set back from the road was a brick house with white columns. It was big all right. But it was the only one in sight. It looked lonesome sitting all by itself. Beyond it stretched a field of mud. Nothing but mud. There was no lake, no grass, no flowers, not a single tree.

"Where are the other houses?" her mother said.

"Where's the pool?" Nancy asked. "And the fitness spa?"

"I don't see a sandbox." JoJo had brought along her pail and shovel. "Mommy, you said there was a playground."

"Well, in a couple of years maybe there will be." Nancy's dad looked annoyed.

Her mom said, "Everything we read makes it sound as if there are finished houses and you could move in tomorrow."

"That's false advertising. It's misleading the consumer," Nancy informed her parents. She knew this because of Bree, whose father made TV commercials. "A consumer," she explained to her sister, "is a person who wants to buy something."

"Well, this consumer has seen enough," her dad said. "Let's go."

But before they were back in the car, they heard a man's voice calling to them. "Wait! Don't leave. You must be the Clancys."

They all turned.

A white-haired man with a jolly smile was standing at the door of the big white house. "I've been expecting you. I'm Eugene. The tour guide for Crystal Lake Estates. Come in, please. See our beautiful model home."

"Thanks, but no thanks," her dad said.

"I need to pee," JoJo said.

So that settled it.

JoJo took care of business in the hall powder room. When she was done, Nancy peeked in. The wallpaper had zebra stripes. The sink had gold faucets. As for the living room, it was nearly as big as the whole downstairs of the Clancys' house. All the furniture was modern and *très* glamorous.

42

Nancy couldn't help being impressed.

In the den, Eugene encouraged her dad to try out the black leather recliner.

As her father lay back in it, he pressed the setting for a back rub.

"Oh, I could get used to this," he said, smiling and vibrating.

Nancy's mother, however, was still annoyed. "I spoke to someone in the managing office," she told Eugene. "Twice, in fact. I heard all about the great deals for the first people who buy houses. Nobody ever said that it's just a construction site."

"Really? I'm sorry about that. Truly. All I do is give tours on the weekend," Eugene said.

Nancy's mother's face softened. "I know it's not your fault. I don't mean to take it out on—"

Her mother never finished the sentence. Suddenly she put one hand on her tummy and clapped her other hand over her mouth. Her eyes darted around and when they landed on the powder room, she made a dash for it.

"Mommy's throwing up!" JoJo said.

There was no need for an announcement. Everyone could hear.

When her mother came out, there was a weak smile on her face. "My goodness. I didn't plan on that happening."

Dad sat her down on one of the living room sofas. Eugene kept apologizing because he couldn't get her a glass of water. All the kitchen cabinets were empty. "I have a handkerchief. Let me dampen it with cold water for your forehead."

"No. I'm fine. I'm fine." Nancy's mom hated for anyone to make a fuss over her. "Breakfast must not have agreed with me."

When she felt well enough, the Clancys

thanked Eugene and started for home.
Nancy never even had a chance to see the
upstairs of the house with the bedroom

and private bathroom that might have been hers. Then, in the next second, Nancy realized that the Clancys were not moving. Not to Crystal Lake Estates anyway. Nancy was safe. At least for now. This was superb news and she couldn't wait to tell it to Bree.

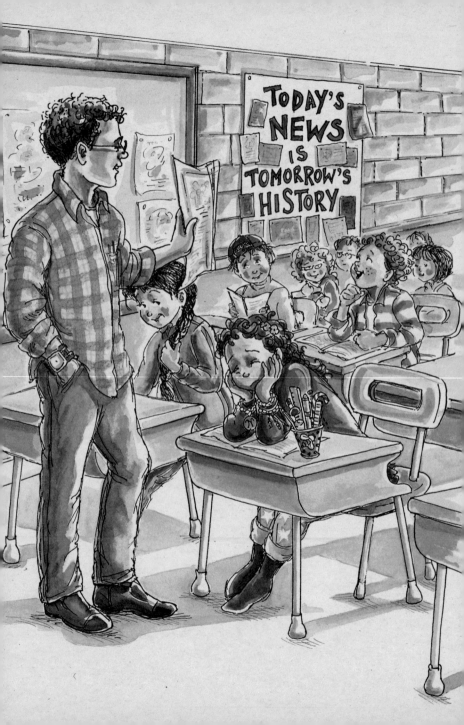

CHAPTER 5

LISTENING IN

The following day, Mr. Dudeny sent Nancy to the nurse's office. She didn't want to go. It meant missing art class. She was almost finished making a clay unicorn. However, all morning long, her eyes had been burning and her tummy felt funny.

In social studies she could barely keep

herself from putting her head on her desk.

Mr. Dudeny was talking about the town paper. He'd brought in a copy. "Just like the *Third Grade Gazette,* our paper focuses on local news. Events that are important to our community. Like this," he said. Then he began reading aloud an article that had to do with building permits and how the town wasn't giving them out, which made people very angry and . . . On and on he read. Words, words, and more words. They swam around in Nancy's head, making her dizzy.

Suddenly she heard Bree saying, "Mr. Dudeny, that's the place Nancy and her family saw!"

"What?" Nancy said. She didn't bother turning toward Bree. It hurt too much to move her eyeballs.

"Crystal Lake Estates! Nancy went there on Sunday," Bree told the class. "The houses aren't built yet. Tell them, Nancy."

Nancy didn't have the energy to speak.

Mr D put down the paper and was now looking intently at Nancy. He came over to her desk.

"You're not yourself today, are you?" Mr. D said, sounding concerned. Then he sent Nancy on her way to the nurse's office.

Mrs. Bergman was pouring a capful of mouthwash for a little boy who'd lost a tooth during recess. While he was rinsing and spitting, Nancy said what was bothering her.

Mrs. Bergman kept nodding. "You rest for a while on the cot. And here, take this," she said, and handed Nancy a blanket. "There's a nasty bug going around."

"I think my mom caught it. Yesterday she regurgitated."

"Well, you let me know if you think you're going to."

Nancy nodded. A thermometer was under her tongue. And sure enough she had a fever. Then before she knew it, she dozed off.

* * *

Nancy didn't know how much later it was when she heard Mrs. Bergman saying, "Nancy, your father will be here shortly to take you home."

Nancy sat up. Her head spun. "I need my backpack. It's in my classroom," she said groggily.

Mrs. Bergman checked her watch. "It's still recess. Nobody's there to bring it down for you. Do you feel well enough to go get it?"

Nancy nodded.

It felt as if weights were in her shoes as she trudged upstairs to her classroom.

The door was open a crack. Mr. D was inside. Nancy could hear him talking. No one was answering, so he had to be on the phone. Nancy didn't know whether to knock or stay waiting in the hall.

"Yeah, you know, it's something I've been thinking about for—oh, I don't know. At least a year," Mr. Dudeny said.

This sounded like an important

conversation. It wouldn't be polite, would it, to barge in? Nancy remained at the door, unsure what to do.

"Yeah, of course it'll be hard after being here so long."

Nancy didn't mean to eavesdrop. But it was impossible not to hear.

There was a long moment of silence. Nancy was scared Mr. Dudeny knew she was outside and any second now was going to fling open the door and find her. But no. He must have been listening to the person on the other end of the line.

Finally he said, "I'm glad that you agree it's the right decision. Of course, I'm sure going to miss them. A lot. But like I keep telling myself—time for a change."

More silence.

"No. I can't wait until June. Yeah, it is too bad. But I have to leave by the end of the month."

Again more silence.

"Okay. Listen, gotta go. The kids will be back from recess any minute. Later, dude."

Evidently, the conversation was over.

What did it mean, all the stuff about "leaving" and "missing them" and "time for a change"? Nancy felt too sick for her brain to make sense of anything. She waited a nanosecond, then rapped hard on the classroom door. "It's me, Mr. D. Nancy."

"Come on in."

She barely had time to grab her backpack before her tummy did a cartwheel.

Nancy dashed out of the classroom and made it to the girls' room just in time to regurgitate.

* * *

At home, Nancy slept all afternoon. When she woke up, she felt a little better. Her eyeballs weren't on fire anymore. Her head had stopped throbbing.

She sat up. Above her, in the attic, she could hear her mom, dad, and JoJo clomping around.

Nancy went down the hall, where the ladder to the attic was pulled down.

"Guys! What's going on up there?" she called.

"We're finding old stuff!" JoJo shouted. "Look! Daddy made this!" JoJo peered down at Nancy through the open trapdoor.

She tossed down a gigantic ball made of rubber bands.

"Careful with that!" Nancy heard her father say. "That's a precious memento from my college days."

A moment later, JoJo scrambled backward down the ladder, followed by Nancy's

mom, who waited at the bottom while Nancy's dad handed down carton after carton. They were marked *Baby Clothes*, *Baby Toys*, and *Baby Books*.

Nancy's mother explained, "A couple we know are expecting a baby and can use all this."

"Ooh! Can I look at the clothes before you give them away?" Nancy asked.

Back in her room, while she and Mom sipped ginger ale and munched on saltine crackers, Nancy took out all the tiny, carefully folded clothes and lay them on her bed. In spite of all the photos she'd seen of herself as a baby, Nancy still found it impossible to believe she'd once been small enough to wear what looked like doll clothes. And, no surprise, they were awfully plain looking. Baby dresses and shorts and overalls and T-shirts all in solid colors. Not a polka dot or flower print to be seen.

Then at the bottom of one carton she unearthed a little strawberry-pink tutu. "Ooh la la! Adorable."

Her mom smiled. "You chose that your-self. We were in a store. You saw it. And you wanted it. I mean you *really* wanted it. You couldn't have been more than two."

This came as no surprise to Nancy. It was obvious that she had been born with exquisite taste.

"Mom, you can't give the tutu away! Someday it will be a precious memento of my childhood."

Her mom laughed. "Well, if your father

gets to keep that ridiculous ball of rubber bands, then you get to keep your first
tutu."

When they were almost finished repack-
ing all the baby clothes, the bell outside
Nancy's window rang.

Bree was sending over Nancy's homework assignment for the next day. It was

to read an editorial in the local newspaper. In an editorial, Mr. Dudeny had explained, a writer expressed their personal opinion about an important news event.

Chérie, I hope you're feeling better, Bree had written in plain English (and a little French), not pig Latin. Homework didn't count as a secret message.

Bree! Suddenly Nancy flashed back to Mr. Dudeny's mysterious phone call. How could she have forgotten? Nancy needed to discuss every word with Bree *tout de suite*. In French that meant pronto. Nancy turned to her mother. "Bree has to come over. Right now. It's an emergency!"

"I don't want you spreading germs," Mom said. "You can call Bree."

No, not good enough. This was a

conversation that needed to take place face-to-face. "What if Bree stays out in the hallway? I give you my solemn word that I won't let her step foot in my room."

"*Wel-l-l . . .*"

That sounded like a "yes" to Nancy.

"*Merci*, Mom!"

Nancy sent a message back, and moments later Bree was sitting cross-legged outside the door to Nancy's bedroom.

As best she could, Nancy recounted the mysterious phone call. "It was about Mr. D leaving someplace," she said. "It made him sad but he said it was 'time for a change.' And the change is going to come soon. Before next month. He said he wanted to wait till June but couldn't."

The whole time she was listening to

Nancy, Bree kept nodding slowly and tapping her lip. Nancy could tell Bree was pondering. She was thinking really hard.

Nancy waited patiently.

Bree tapped her lip some more. But finally she shrugged and said, "Sorry. I don't have a clue."

Weirdly, right as Bree said this, something clicked in Nancy's brain. It was as if a bunch of scattered jigsaw puzzle pieces moved themselves around and suddenly fit together.

Nancy jumped up, nearly knocking over the empty glass of ginger ale on her nightstand. "*Sacre bleu!* What if Mr. D is leaving Draezel?"

Bree looked confused. "What makes you say that?"

"Think about it." Nancy started ticking off the reasons on her fingers. "Number one: he said he wants a big change in his life. Quitting teaching—that'd be big. Number two: he said he was sorry about leaving in a month. That'd be before school ends. Of

course he'd feel bad doing that. And number three: he talked about 'missing them' so much. All the 'great memories' he had. I think 'them' means us! Our class!"

Nancy flopped back on her bed. Her head had started pounding again. She covered her eyes. "I finally uncovered major news. And it's awful. There's nobody like Mr. D! Nobody!"

"I don't know, Nancy." Bree was shaking her head slowly. "The phone call could mean lots of things." Bree stood. "You only heard one side. You may be jumping to conclusions."

Nancy sat up. "I heard what I heard. Facts are facts."

"I know. But you have to make sure of what the facts mean," Bree went on. "It's called verifying information. Remember?"

"Yes, Bree. I know that," Nancy said. Verifying facts was something every reporter did, Mr. D had explained to the class. It was to make sure that their story was accurate. Nancy stared at Bree. She was growing . . . not annoyed, exactly. But she felt let down. She had expected Bree to act just as upset as she was.

"There's one small problem, Bree. The only way I can verify stuff is to ask Mr. Dudeny if he's leaving. How can I do that? I only found out because I was eavesdropping."

"True. But maybe there's another way," said Bree. She began tapping her lip again. "I wish we were in the clubhouse. I think better there."

"Me too," Nancy said, and since refreshments—even saltines—also helped with pondering, she and Bree sat on opposite sides of the doorway passing the

almost-empty box of crackers back and forth.

Sure enough, before too long they managed to come up with a plan.

Nancy was going to ask if she could interview Mr. D for the next issue of the *Third Grade Gazette*. If he said yes, she would ask lots of leading questions, questions that might make Mr. Dudeny open up on his own about his "big change."

"And remember," Bree said, "keep it secret, what you heard."

"Of course," Nancy said. "I have no intention of revealing a word."

CHAPTER **6**

BLABBING

The following morning, even before her regular wake-up time, Nancy was dressed and downstairs for breakfast. She was determined to return to school.

"I feel fine. And I won't breathe on anybody," Nancy promised.

Since she didn't have a fever, her

parents let her go.

It was a normal day at school. Or as normal as it could be, knowing Mr. D might be leaving. Nancy felt sad every time Mr. D did some typical Mr. D thing, like cracking his knuckles or tipping way back in his chair with his hands behind his head. Nancy felt as if she were already missing him even though he was there right in front of her.

Before lunch, Nancy went up to Mr. Dudeny. "I'd really like to interview you for the *Gazette*. I think our readers would be fascinated to learn more about you."

"Of course. I'm very flattered!" Mr. D said. They set up a time—library period— the next day.

Nancy and Bree spent all of lunch

deciding on the best questions to ask.

"Maybe I could ask what his dreams for the future are," Nancy said, peeling a banana. She still didn't have much appetite.

"That's pretty good."

"It'll seem like an innocent question," Nancy went on, "but it might catch him off guard and—who knows? He might tell me everything."

Grace and Clara were setting down their trays at the table.

As soon as Grace found out about the interview, she looked mad that she hadn't thought of it first. Then right away she started telling Nancy what to ask. "Find out how much money he makes and who is his favorite kid in the class."

"Grace, he's not going to answer that," Clara said.

Grace shrugged. "Well, at least try to find out some personal stuff."

"Like what? We know he's not married," Clara said.

"Nancy could say, 'Is there a special someone in your life?' When stars are interviewed on TV, they always get asked that."

Nancy had to admit, it was a pretty good question. She added it to the list.

That afternoon, Bree had her tap-dance lesson, so after school Nancy lay in the clubhouse hammock trying to come up with more interview questions. She had ten. Was there anything she'd missed? She'd never interviewed anyone before and she wanted to be professional. Then, it came over Nancy again. The real reason for the interview. In a few weeks, Mr. Dudeny might be gone from their lives forever! There'd be a new teacher in 3D. A stranger sitting at his desk. Mr.

D's poster of Dire Straits—his favorite band—would be gone and so would his mug that said *MUG* in big letters. It was too sad to contemplate!

"Knock, knock," Nancy heard someone saying.

It was Clara.

She pulled aside the old sheet that served as the entrance to their club-house.

"Your mom said you were out here. I was just riding by."

Nancy invited her in and let Clara look over the list of questions.

"Ooh. 'What were you like as a kid?' That's a fun one." Clara stopped. "Nancy, what's wrong? You look so sad."

Nancy swallowed hard. "It's nothing,"

she managed to say.

Clara came over and wiggled beside Nancy in the hammock. She slung an arm around her shoulder. "Come on. Whatever it is, you can tell me."

Nancy tried to smile. Clara was such a kind person. Someone who was easy to confide in. Before she could stop herself, Nancy blurted out everything.

Clara's eyes grew wider and wider while she listened. She looked stunned. "This— this is just horrible news!" she sputtered. "I'll miss him so much. Oh! And my poor little sister. All I do is say how great he is. Now she won't get him next year for third grade."

"Clara, promise you won't tell anybody. Not a soul."

"I promise." Clara pretended to lock her lips and throw away the key. Then she asked, "Does Bree know?"

Nancy nodded.

"Do I know what?"

Bree still had on her tap shoes and a blue leotard with a short, flouncy skirt around it. She was standing at the club- house entrance.

"About Mr. D leaving! It's so horrible," Clara said.

"Don't worry, Bree. Clara's not going to tell a soul," Nancy added quickly. "Isn't that right, Clara?"

Bree didn't see Clara nodding. She had already spun around and left.

Later a message arrived in the mail basket. Nancy deciphered it. That meant she translated it from pig Latin into regular English.

You weren't supposed to tell anybody till you had all the facts, Bree had written.

Nancy didn't write back. What was there to say? Bree was right.

* * *

The next day, Bree was still kind of annoyed. "A reporter is supposed to keep stuff confidential."

They were on their way to the art studio.

"Forgive me. It was a moment of weakness and I regret it."

"Okay, forgiven. You're only human."

They walked the rest of the way arm in arm. "It'll be okay as long as Clara keeps quiet."

All during art Nancy concentrated on putting the final touches on her unicorn. Getting the horn to stay on straight was tricky but kept her from thinking about the interview. It was next period.

Then, what seemed like only a second later, the bell rang. Nancy's throat went dry. She swallowed hard. "I'm nervous," she told Bree.

Bree hugged her, told Nancy she'd do great, and headed toward the library while Nancy returned to the classroom.

Mr. D was at his desk, drinking tea from the mug that said *MUG*. "Have a seat and fire away," he told Nancy.

From her first questions Nancy learned many superb facts.

Mr. Dudeny was the youngest of six children.

All his sisters and brothers still called him Pip—short for Pip-squeak.

Maple walnut was his favorite flavor of ice cream.

He loved horror movies—the scarier the better.

He could surf.

Then Nancy decided it was time to move on to her leading questions. She cleared her throat.

"Did you always know you wanted to be a teacher?"

He shook his head. "After college, I worked in Philadelphia at a bookstore.

Then I drove a cab for a while in Chicago. After that I moved to Florida and was a lifeguard. I'm a restless guy. I like having new experiences."

Nancy stopped herself from frowning. That wasn't a reassuring answer.

Having new experiences meant leaving old experiences—like teaching—behind.

"What made you become a teacher?" she asked next.

"When I was a lifeguard, I taught swimming classes. I realized how much I enjoy being around kids. Doing what I do now means I'm around kids all day."

Ooh la la! This answer was a lot better! "Well, it certainly sounds like you found the right profession!" Nancy said.

"Yes, I think I have," he said. "Draezel is a superb school."

Nancy liked the

sound of that answer too. Her body started to relax.

"So that means you'll never leave here."

"Oh, I don't know about that." Mr. Dudeny smiled. "Like I said, I get restless."

No! Wrong answer! Nancy stared down at her notepad. The correct answer to the last question was: Mr. Dudeny planned to stay at Draezel forever and ever. Until he retired.

Nancy realized that she was getting nowhere. It was as if she were being spun in a circle or playing a confusing board game where, just when she thought she was about to win, it turned out she was right back at square one.

Another question popped into her head, one that wasn't on her list but one that might pin down Mr. Dudeny more.

On the phone Mr. Dudeny had said the big change was coming in a month. Room 3D's next class trip was also in a month.

"Are you excited about the next class trip?" Nancy asked. The third and fourth grades were going to a matinee—an afternoon performance—of *Peter Pan*. Mr. D had arranged it.

Pen poised, Nancy waited to hear Mr. D say: "It will be one of the most superb moments of the school year."

Instead he went and rinsed his *MUG* mug in the sink. When he sat back down he said, "Unfortunately, Nancy, I won't be able to go. Something's come up. But you'll all still have a great time without me."

No. No, we won't! Nancy wanted to say,

"Don't leave. School won't be any fun without you."

Mr. D glanced at his watch. "So? Anything else you want to ask?"

"I guess I have all I need to know."

CHAPTER 7

NEWS TRAVELS FAST

"How'd it go?" Bree asked as soon as Nancy arrived in the library. Then she looked at Nancy's face. "Oh no! Did he say he's leaving?"

"Almost. He told me he can't go to *Peter Pan*. He didn't say why. Just that 'something's come up.'"

"Ew." Bree made a face as if she smelled something rotten. "I don't like the sound of that."

"Girls, less talking, please." Mr. Binder was looking their way. He held up two fingers pointing in opposite directions. So Bree went over to the new arrivals book cart and Nancy looked through the mystery shelf. Even finding a Nancy Drew she hadn't read—*Password to Larkspur Lane*—didn't do anything to lift her spirits.

There was a tap on her shoulder. She turned.

It was Robert.

"Is it true?" he whispered.

"Is what true?"

"About Mr. D leaving?"

Nancy's eyes widened. "Clara told you?"

"Yes. She was looking really unhappy. I asked her what was wrong."

"Listen, Robert. Promise you won't tell anybody else! It's not for sure, anyway."

Robert promised.

Nancy found Clara by the window in an armchair, reading.

"You told Robert!" Nancy hissed under her breath. "I trusted you, Clara. You locked your lips and everything."

"I'm sorry!" she whispered, clutching Nancy's arm. "I didn't mean to tell, Nancy. Honest. It just sort of slipped out."

"Well, *merci beaucoup*," Nancy whispered back angrily. She started to march off. But tears were beginning to run down Clara's cheeks.

"Listen, Clara. Don't cry," Nancy said

with a sigh. It wasn't fair, was it, to get mad at Clara for blabbing when Nancy had blabbed herself. Keeping big news a secret was hard. "You didn't tell anybody else, did you?"

Clara's eyes shifted away from Nancy. She didn't reply.

"Oh, Clara!"

"I didn't tell anybody else. I swear. But Grace was nearby when I told Robert. She might have been listening."

Grace! Grace's ears had superpower hearing. This was way beyond bad. It was horrendous!

Just as Nancy feared, the news was spreading like wildfire.

A kid from the other third grade class came up to Nancy while she was waiting in the cafeteria line.

He knew.

So did Nola and Lionel.

"We heard from Yoko," Lionel said. He looked angry. "I'm supposed to be your good friend. How come you told other kids and didn't tell me?" He stalked off, without bothering to wait for an answer.

Nancy took her lunch tray over to her regular table. Bree was already there. Nancy felt torn. Should she tell Bree what was going on? Bree was going to say, "I told you so."

It turned out that Nancy didn't have to tell Bree.

"I found this in my 'Just Ask Bree' mailbox." She was holding a note. She let Nancy read it.

Dear Bree,

I am very upset. There's a rumor going around that my teacher is leaving school really soon. I don't know what to do. Is it okay to ask him if it's true?

Thank you,

Confused

Before Nancy could utter a word, Grace passed by. "Did you hear? Mr. Dudeny is leaving next week."

"No!" Nancy cried. "He never said that."

"He keeps saying what a great class we are. But he's deserting us!" Grace went on. "Teachers have to sign contracts, you know. Maybe he can be sued. Both my parents are lawyers. They'll know."

Nancy put her head in her hands. If only time were like a computer and she could press the delete button, erase the last couple of days and start them over again. She felt Bree's arm wrap around her shoulder.

"I never meant for this to happen," Nancy wailed. "I'll never forgive myself if I get Mr. D in trouble. What should I do?"

Right away Bree came up with sensible advice: "Tell your parents."

CLEANING UP
A MESS

When Nancy got home, she found her dad doing the cha-cha in the living room with JoJo on his shoulders. Her mom was also dancing, holding Frenchy's front paws.

"We're not moving!" JoJo cried. "Our house is getting bigger."

97

Nancy's mom let go of Frenchy's paws. "We're going to build an addition! So"— she made an abracadabra motion with her hand—"problem solved!"

"That's nice," Nancy said flatly, and threw herself on the sofa.

Her dad stopped doing the cha-cha. He put JoJo down. "Nice? That's all? I was expecting screams of joy."

"Are you feeling sick again, honey?" Nancy's mom asked. She came over and pressed the back of her hand against Nancy's forehead.

"I'm not sick. I'm okay."

Then her dad explained about the good news. It had to do with getting a building permit from the town council. "We applied months ago but they took their sweet time," he said. "The permit finally came in the mail today."

"It's what we wanted all along," her mom added. "We never wanted to move, and now we don't have to. We can build an annex—doesn't that sound fancy? There'll be an office for Dad and an extra room too so—"

"Mom! Dad! Stop!" Nancy held up a hand like a traffic cop. "I need to tell you something! I'm scared Mr. Dudeny may get in trouble. All because of me." Nancy started crying now. Crying hard. "I think he's leaving Draezel. I heard some stuff he said on the phone. I let it get out and now everybody knows. Everybody! Grace's parents are going to sue!"

"Whoa! Whoa! Whoa! Slow down," her

dad said. "Take a couple of deep breaths."

So Nancy did.

"Nancy, did you do something bad?" JoJo asked. She looked both worried and excited.

"JoJo," Dad said. "I have an idea. Why don't you go outside and play with Frenchy in the yard?"

"No. I want to hear." JoJo plopped down on the rug while Nancy's parents, sitting on either side of her, listened to everything that had happened since Nancy heard Mr. D on the phone.

At the end, her dad said, "Okay. So the trouble started because you were eavesdropping?"

Nancy nodded.

"Which you know is wrong. It was a

private conversation," her mom said. "And then you let a story get out, which, even if it's true, wasn't your story to tell."

Nancy nodded again. "I'm a terrible girl."

"No, you're a wonderful girl who made some mistakes." Her mom wrapped both arms around Nancy.

The warm, spicy scent of her mother—it was a special Mom smell that didn't come from any perfume—instantly comforted Nancy. She stopped crying. All she wanted was to remain with her face buried in her mother's neck.

"Also, maybe you're wrong about Mr. Dudeny," her dad said.

"Really? You think?" Nancy turned so she was facing her father.

"To me, it seems like you put two and

two together without any proof that it was going to add up to four."

"What else could it mean, Dad?" Nancy untangled herself from Mom and swiped at her leaky nose.

"I don't know. Any number of things. There's only one way to find out."

Nancy was pretty sure what was coming next. She watched her dad get the school directory from the desk. "Here's his number. You need to call Mr. Dudeny and tell him what's going on. You'll work it out from there." He handed her his phone.

Strangely, even though Nancy was terrified to call, she felt a sense of relief. Her parents were solving the problem. They were helping her clean up the mess she'd made.

Before Nancy could dial, JoJo jumped

into her lap. She cupped Nancy's face in her hands. They were sticky. Then she kissed her and said, "It's okay. I make mistakes too. You'll do better next time."

CHAPTER **9**

NO NEWS IS GREAT NEWS

"Leaving Draezel? No! What gave you that idea?" After he heard why, Mr. Dudeny told Nancy that his "big change" was moving to his own apartment.

"I've been sharing a house with some college buddies. A great bunch of guys. But I want my own place."

Also, it turned out that the reason for Mr. D missing *Peter Pan* was that a friend's van, one big enough for moving furniture, was only available on the day of the class trip.

"So you overheard me on the phone."

"Yes. I'm so sorry. Really! I didn't mean to. Not at first. Then I didn't want you to know I was listening. I was afraid you'd get mad."

"I wouldn't have been happy about it, but we could've settled everything right away."

"I know. And I made it worse because—" Nancy paused. The next part was even harder to tell. "Well, I told a couple of kids . . . and they told more kids."

Mr. Dudeny didn't reply. Maybe he was

pondering. Finally he said, "So I guess this explains the message I got to call Grace's mother."

"*Sacre bleu!* Really?"

"Well, now I know why she called and what to say. And don't worry. I'll keep your name out of it. But Nancy—"

"Yes, Mr. Dudeny?"

"Do you know what inquisitive means?"

"Yes. It means curious."

"Exactly. You're an inquisitive girl with lots of imagination. Those are superb qualities to have."

Normally Nancy would have said *merci beaucoup*, except she could hear there was a "but" coming next. "But," he continued, "this time you let your imagination run away from you. You misinterpreted everything that I said. You made yourself unhappy and some other kids too. All for no reason."

"I know that. And . . ." Nancy looked for words to express just how sorry she was. "And I apologize profusely," she said.

"Apology accepted. I'll say something to the whole class tomorrow. In the meantime, you can let your friends know this was nothing more than a big misunderstanding."

This time Nancy did say *merci beaucoup*. And then she told Mr. Dudeny how ecstatic—how super-duper happy—she was that he was staying at Ada M. Draezel Elementary School.

Nancy got off the phone. That's when she saw JoJo, who had been hiding by the sofa, listening. But Nancy didn't get mad at JoJo for eavesdropping. Instead, she grabbed her sister's hands and started doing the cha-cha. Who knew? If JoJo was lucky, by the time she got to third grade, Mr. Dudeny would still be in room 3D. With the Dire Straits poster on the wall. And the mug that said *MUG* on his desk.

email

To: All students in 3D
From: Nancy Clancy
Subject: Our beloved teacher

Dear Members of Room 3D,

Because of me, a rumor started that Mr. Dudeny was leaving Draezel. I was mistaken. Please accept my heartfelt apology.

Yours sincerely,
Nancy Clancy

CHAPTER 10

THE BIGGEST NEWS OF ALL

As soon as she woke up, Nancy swallowed a few times, testing to see whether her throat was sore. If it was, then she could stay home and avoid everybody at school. But her throat felt fine.

"Look, honey. Sure, kids are going to ask about the email," Mom said at the kitchen table, spreading peanut butter on an English muffin for JoJo. "And you'll feel embarrassed. But you don't need to go into a long story. Just say again that you're sorry. Believe me: after today, it will blow over and be forgotten."

"Your mother is a wise woman," her dad added. "There's nothing as stale as yesterday's news."

Her mom nodded. "Exactly. What seems like a big deal now won't be for long."

"I wish this day was over," Nancy said, shouldering her backpack.

"It won't be so bad," Bree said a little while later as they walked to school. "I'm right here to stick up for you."

Sure enough, even before they reached the classroom, Grace came hurrying over

to Nancy. "Don't you feel dumb for starting a big rumor?" Several other kids from
3D were in the hallway. They all stopped
to listen.

"Cut it out, Grace," Bree said. "Nancy
just . . ."

Nancy didn't let Bree finish. "Yes, I do
feel dumb," she said to Grace. "I'm sorry it
happened."

"So why'd you do it?" Grace tailed after
them into room 3D. "Is Mr. D talking to
you?"

"I misunderstood something that he
said. That's all. I didn't mean to start trouble. Mr. D knows and he's forgiven me.
Now if you'll excuse me." Nancy shrugged
off her backpack and took her seat. "That's
all I have to say."

Bree gave Nancy a thumbs-up.

Mr. D waited until everyone was at their desks. Then he said, "I guess some of you have heard that I'm moving to a new apartment. Once I've settled in, you'll all be invited to a housewarming party. I'd love any of your artwork. There's lots of wall space."

Right away Nancy knew the perfect gift for Mr. D. Not a painting—but her clay unicorn.

* * *

Her parents were right. A day later, every-thing at school went back to normal. The rumor was forgotten. Other news took its place. Clara came in with a short new haircut. Lionel got braces with little rubber bands that he could twang and shoot out of his mouth.

Also that week, building started on the annex. Over the next month, as the Clancys' house got bigger, their yard got smaller.

On most days after school, Nancy and Bree watched the workmen putting up the frame. It looked like something made from a giant set of Legos. Soon the walls went up; the floors were down and the annex was starting to look real.

Nancy's parents pointed out where her dad's office would go, as well as a new bedroom with a bathroom. It was going to be Nancy's. Her own private bathroom! She could scarcely believe it.

"Can it have gold faucets on the sink

and zebra-stripe wallpaper like at that
model house?" Nancy asked. "And maybe
towels with my initials!"

"Those decisions will be made at a later
date," her mother said, which told Nancy
that the answer was no. It was dinnertime
and Mom was serving herself a generous

second helping of meat loaf.

Lately, Nancy had noticed, her mother seemed hungry all the time. Perhaps she was making up for all those weeks when she hadn't had any appetite and lived on saltines.

"However," Mom added, spooning more mashed potatoes onto her plate, "your room and bathroom may be whatever color you want."

* * *

At the hardware store, Nancy selected dozens of paint chips to take home. They were free. They were gorgeous. She and Bree spent hours poring over them. The choices were endless. Should her new room be flamingo pink or sunflower yellow or perhaps seafoam blue? In the end she settled on a color called twilight, which was a beautiful shade of purple. Just a little darker than lavender.

As for the bathroom, Nancy wanted it to be white with polka dots that she'd paint on herself in the same purple as her room. "It'll look very coordinated," Nancy told Bree, which meant everything would go together perfectly. And her mother agreed to new matching towels, but ones without her initials.

The day the workers started painting was the same day Nancy came home with the next issue of the *Third Grade Gazette*. Nancy's interview with Mr. D appeared on the front page. The bottom half of it.

"The *Gazette*! The *Gazette*! It's here!" she shouted as she burst into the house.

But the only people to hear her were Mrs. DeVine and JoJo. They were playing Candyland.

"Where's Mom?" Nancy asked.

"She had a doctor appointment. Your father's meeting her there."

"What? Is something wrong? Is Mom okay?" Nancy asked.

"I'm sure she's fine," Mrs. DeVine said, turning over the card for Ice Cream Raft. "She said it was just a checkup."

But why, then, had her dad bothered going? That was unusual. His boss, Mr. Castle, never liked him leaving work early.

A short while later, her parents returned home. As Mrs. DeVine waved good-bye, Mom took Nancy's hand and steered her into the living room while Dad scooped up JoJo. They all sat on the sofa.

"We have some big news!" her mother announced.

It sure was. It was bigger than big. It

was ginormous news!

Nancy tried to take it all in. The news explained a lot of things, like why her mom hadn't been feeling well a while ago. Like why her family needed more room—it wasn't just for her dad's office. And why her parents had taken down all the baby stuff from the attic. Their friends didn't need baby clothes. The Clancys did!

JoJo was sitting on Dad's lap. She looked puzzled. "Mommy's having a baby?" she asked.

"Babies, JoJo, babies!" Nancy's father corrected. "We're going to have twins! The doctor is sure."

JoJo, however, didn't look sure about this. "I like it the way we are."

"But JoJo. You finally get to be a big

sister," Nancy pointed out.

Hearing that, JoJo looked much happier.

"And I," Nancy suddenly realized, "won't only be an older sister. I'll be the eldest of four!"

A strange warm feeling had seized hold of Nancy and was spreading all through her. She felt almost as if she were glowing. Twins! Twins with tiny ears, tiny noses, tiny fingers, tiny toes. Tiny everything! It was too adorable for words. They could share her little tutu! Nancy hardly remembered JoJo as a baby. Nancy had been too young. But now she was almost ten. "I can feed them and dress them and rock them to sleep!"

"I want that in writing," Dad said.

The babies would be born six months from now, Nancy found out. And no, her parents had not given any thought to names.

"No plain ones, please. Maybe their names could be French? Like Françoise and Felice or Elise and . . ."

"Well, those are nice names," her mother said. "But they're for girls . . . and the doctor . . . Well, he's pretty sure they're boys."

JoJo started squealing. "They can be my posse!"

Suddenly Nancy's visions of miniature pinafores and sunbonnets and party dresses vanished. "Oh!" was all she said. Then she thought to herself: babies were babies. She would love them anyway. And there were plenty of French boy names.

"I'm still overjoyed," she said. Then in the next breath, she asked if she could tell Bree.

"Absolutely. It's not a secret anymore."

Before her mother had even finished the sentence, Nancy was already out the door to share what, so far in all her nine and a half years on this planet, was the biggest, most unexpected news of her life. A new chapter was about to begin.

Six months later:

Claire, Doug, Nancy, and JoJo Clancy
are thrilled to announce the birth of

Robert Antoine and Edward Pierre
May 6

A CHAPTER BOOK SERIES STARRING EVERYONE'S FAVORITE FANCY GIRL

HARPER
An Imprint of HarperCollinsPublishers

www.fancynancyworld.com